D0783868

BEST-LOVED
SWIFT

JONATHAN SWIFT was born in Dublin in 1667, and educated at Kilkenny College and Trinity College, Dublin. At first he divided his time between Ireland and England, where he became a political spin doctor, advising Queen Anne and her ministers. In Ireland he was rector of two rural parishes, and, from 1713 until his death in 1745, was Dean of St Patrick's Cathedral, Dublin.

Swift's inner life was a private and perhaps tortured one, but he had close relationships with two women – 'Stella' and 'Vanessa' – both of whom came from England to be near him in Dublin. His verses about them are often witty and moving, though in other works about women, he appears to have been repelled by their physicality.

But it was not just women that disgusted Swift. Mankind in general disappointed him; he portrayed human greed, venality and stupidity in terms so shocking and direct that many of his works, including the extraordinary, many-layered *Gulliver's Travels*, had to be published anonymously. His pamphleteering on behalf of the Irish made him a hero, loved by the Dublin poor. For the precision of his prose, the humour and honesty of his poems, and the power of his imagination, he remains essential reading today.

JOHN WYSE JACKSON was born in Kilkenny in 1953 and educated in Dublin. His previous books include *Best-Loved Oscar Wilde*, *We All Want to Change the World: A Life of John Lennon*, *Dublin: Poetry of Place* and, with Peter Costello, *John Stanislaus Joyce: The Voluminous Life of James Joyce's Father*. He has edited two volumes of the writings of Flann O'Brien (Myles na gCopaleen) and, with the artist Hector McDonnell, three books of light verse, including *Ireland's Other Poetry: Anonymous to Zozimus*. He lives with his family in County Wexford, and welcomes visitors to his second-hand bookshop, Zozimus Bookshop, at 86 Main Street, Gorey.

BEST-LOVED

SWIFT

BEING

A Selection of

VERSES & PROSE

And

NOTES HISTORICAL AND EXPLANATORY

Arrang'd, Revised and Edited by

Mr. Jno Wyse Jackson

Adorned with

COPPER-PLATES

Printed for The O'Brien Press

DUBLIN

MMXVIII

First published 2018 by The O'Brien Press Ltd,
12 Terenure Road East, Rathgar, Dublin 6, D06 HD27, Ireland.
Tel: +353 1 4923333; Fax: +353 1 4922777
E-mail: books@obrien.ie; Website: www.obrien.ie
The O'Brien Press is a member of Publishing Ireland.

ISBN: 978-1-84717-948-7

Every effort has been made to trace copyright holders and to obtain their
permission for the use of copyright material. The publisher apologises for any
errors or omissions and would be grateful if notified of any corrections that
should be incorporated in future reprints or editions of this book.

10 9 8 7 6 5 4 3 2 1
23 22 21 20 19 18

Printed and bound by Gutenberg Press, Malta.
The paper in this book is produced using pulp from managed forests

Published in

In memory of

Terence Moran,

1954–2017.

List of illustrations

TABLE OF CONTENTS

INTRODUCTION

BEING

A Note

HISTORICAL

On the Dean's Life

AND

AN APPRECIATION

of his

Contribution to Society

Jonathan Swift was unique, a one-off — in truth, a sort of freak. Always something of an Irishman in England and an Englishman in Ireland, he was also many other things: a man of warm humour and of bitter gloom, a man of shocking coarseness and of deep Christian faith and practice, a man of considerable moral and physical courage who couldn't tell the truth to the women he loved. He was a consummate political negotiator in London during the time of Queen Anne, and in Ireland was a scourge to all who held power over the people. Though he could often be angry, depressed or mean-minded, his many friendships with both men and women were convivial, and his intimates were captivated by his conversation, which was not just verbally clever, but very funny — rarely the same thing.

Above all, Swift enjoyed a good argument. He was a writer not because he fancied a literary career, but because he wanted to make things happen. 'We all want to change the world,' a later near-Irishman would put it: Swift had a good idea of just how to do that. 'Ink,' he once wrote, 'is the great missive weapon in all battles of the learned, which, conveyed through a sort of engine called a quill, infinite numbers of these are darted at the enemy by the valiant on each side, with equal skill and violence, as if it were an engagement of porcupines.'

In such battles, Swift was rarely on the losing side. His political and historical writings are models of invention, rhetoric and misdirection, all couched in deceptively simple prose that is almost impossible to argue against. Fascinated by the nuts and bolts of language, he was a devastating letter-writer, and a master of satire in both prose and verse.

The Dean's most famous work, *Gulliver's Travels*, in print since the day it was published in 1726, has appeared in countless versions, some with illustrations, some heavily freighted with scholarly apparatus, some expurgated to avoid scandal, some completely rewritten for children. Over the years, many selections and editions of the writer's other works have also been produced for the general reader and, more recently, for the academic market. The earliest compilations reflected the slack practices of the age in matters of literary scholarship, and many pieces printed as Swift's in fact came from other pens. Indeed, some of his best-remembered lines were not written by him at all, such as the following squib – which, being a modern editor, I ought of course to exclude from these pages:

> Behold a proof of Irish sense!
> Here Irish wit is seen!
> When nothing's left that's worth defence,
> We build a magazine.

You may want these lines to be Swift's, but, as Pat Rogers in his brilliant edition of *The Complete Poems* makes evident, they can hardly have been written before the Phoenix Park Magazine Fort was first thought of in 1745. That was the year in which Swift died, long since lost to mental confusion.

But putting witty words into the mouths of the famous is a Dublin sin: it's not so long since it seemed as if every smart remark doing the rounds had allegedly come from the lips of Brendan Behan, Flann O'Brien or Oliver St John Gogarty. The Great Dean of St Patrick's won a similar accolade, in the city and beyond: he became a figure of folklore, whose supposed exploits around the country reached into the Irish language — and this phenomenon lasted until the twentieth century, as Benedict Kiely demonstrated when he recorded these libellous lines in his memoir, *The Waves Behind Us*:

> The Dean of St Patrick's Cathedral
> Flung open his old-fashioned doors,
> And the ghost of Dean Swift
> Toddled forth in his shift
> To the last of the old-fashioned whores.

In reality, the Dean wouldn't have been seen dead with a street prostitute. He was physically fastidious in the extreme, and (for an eighteenth-century man) washed frequently – though in his poems and prose he made repeated, almost canine, returns to the excremental. His love life was secretive, and remains an enigma: two women loved him, his Stella and his Vanessa; it seems likely that he gave different parts of his heart to each of them.

Was Swift an Irish patriot? He said more than once that he hated the land of his birth. He had always wanted to be famous, and resented being rusticated from London's corridors of power to the Deanery in Dublin. As gardener, fisherman and builder of small canals, he was a lover of the Irish countryside, but that didn't blind him to the injustices that were happening in it. In 1719, he wrote his first Irish pamphlet, *A Proposal for the Universal Use of Irish Manufacture*: 'Whoever travels this country, and observes the face of nature, or the faces, and habits, and dwellings of the natives, will hardly think himself in a land where either law, religion, or common humanity is professed.' He was angrily aware that the terrible poverty around him was the fault of English misrule and Irish landlordism.

And by 1724, when he released the fourth of his Drapier Letters (scathing pamphlets that defended the country against the imposition of inferior copper coinage), the question of

Swift's allegiance to the people of Ireland no longer needed to be asked: '... by the laws of GOD, of NATURE, of NATIONS, and of your own country, you ARE and OUGHT to be as FREE a people as your brethren in England.'

Jonathan Swift lived in more spacious days; and to keep this volume a slim one, I have shortened many of the poems and prose pieces here. For variant readings I used the version I liked best, silently updating spellings and punctuation where the sense wasn't affected. I have added brief notes explaining anything I had to look up. The first half of the eighteenth century was a long time ago, and language as old as that usually takes a little getting used to.

With Swift, however, it's not too difficult. His writing bounces along. The poems and prose pieces here tend to be uncomplicated in their language, though they may be intricate in what they express. Some of them will make you laugh, some will make you ponder, and some will make your eyes pop.

One final point: if you happen to read this book from beginning to end, you will find that you are following the story of Jonathan Swift's life, but if you prefer to dip in and out, the outline Chronology (below) may be useful.

John Wyse Jackson

GEARS

CHRONOLOGY

1667   Jonathan Swift is born on 30 November, in Hoey's Court, Dublin.

1668   His nurse kidnaps him, taking him to England for some three years.

1673   Back home, he is sent as a boarder to Kilkenny College.

1682   Enters Trinity College, Dublin, graduating two years later.

1688   William of Orange invades England; James II escapes to France. Civil war in Ireland, so Swift flees to England, where his mother now lives.

1689   Working for Sir William Temple at Moor Park in Surrey; there, tutors the young Esther Johnson ('Stella'). First symptoms of inner ear problems.

1690   Battle of the Boyne. Swift moves to Ireland for his health.

1691   Returns as secretary to Temple's household.

1692   Gets MA degree from Oxford; first poem published.

1694   Back to Ireland to be ordained as Church of Ireland clergyman.

1695   First parish, Kilroot, in rural County Antrim.

1696   Moor Park again. Writing *The Battle of the Books* and *A Tale of a Tub*.

1699   Temple dies. To Ireland with Lord Berkeley, but no political job ensues.

1700   Instituted as Vicar of Laracor, in County Meath; edits Temple's *Letters*.

1701   Publishes his first political pamphlet, supporting the Whigs against the Tories.

1702   Made Doctor of Divinity at Trinity College, Dublin. Stella moves to Dublin with Mrs Dingley.

1704   *A Tale of a Tub* and *The Battle of the Books* published anonymously.

1707	In London for the Church of Ireland, to petition Queen Anne to relieve Irish clerical taxes.
1708	Meets Steele and Addison, and begins writing for the *Tatler* and, later, the *Spectator*. Growing influence in exalted political and literary circles. Rarely in Ireland during these years.
1710	Supports the Tories against the Whigs, writing for their newspaper, the *Examiner*. Begins drinking coffee with Esther Vanhomrigh ('Vanessa') in London. The only letters to Stella in Dublin that are to survive (as *The Journal to Stella*) begin.
1714	Founds the Scriblerus Club with Pope and other writers. The Tory Ministry falls; Queen Anne dies and George I succeeds her. Installed the previous year as Dean of St Patrick's Cathedral, Swift moves finally to live in Ireland, hotly pursued by Vanessa.
1716	Marries Stella (Esther Johnson) in secret; alternatively, doesn't marry anyone at any time.
1719	First Irish political tract, *A Proposal for the Universal Use of Irish Manufacture*, makes waves.
1723	Vanessa dies.
1724	*The Drapier's Letters* castigate the English Government, ultimately forcing a U-turn on the Wood's Halfpence affair. Swift established as a popular hero in Ireland.
1726	*Gulliver's Travels* published to a sensation.
1727	Last stay in England, then back by Holyhead.
1728	Stella dies.
1729	*A Modest Proposal* published.
1735	Publication in Dublin of the first *Collected Works*.
1737	Now seventy, with waning mental abilities, and often ill.
1742	Coherent thought by now scarcely detectable.
1745	19 October: Death of Jonathan Swift.

I.S. Müller inv: del: et Sc:

Part the First:

A TOPSY-TURVY CREATURE.

BEING

An

Introductory Sampler of

EARLY WRITINGS

from the Pen of

Mr. J<u>no</u> Swift

while in the employ of

Sir W<u>m</u> Temple

as

Secretary, Factotum,

&

Tutor to his Household

during the Years of Our Ld.,

1689-1699.

In 1738, towards the end of his career, Swift began trying to write the history of his family. The unfinished manuscript is now preserved in Trinity College, Dublin. A fascinating, though not always accurate, document, it traces the fortunes of some of his more notable forebears, before turning more revealingly to the story of his own parentage and early life (as seen here). The rhythmic first paragraph below is a fine Swiftian riff.

From FRAGMENT OF AUTOBIOGRAPHY

Jonathan Swift, Doctor of Divinity and Dean of St Patrick's ... was born in Dublin, on St. Andrew's day; and when he was a year old, an event happened to him that seems very unusual; for his nurse, who was a woman of Whitehaven, being under an absolute necessity of seeing one of her relations, who was then extremely sick, and from whom she expected a legacy, and being extremely fond of the infant, she stole him on shipboard unknown to his mother and uncle, and carried him with her to Whitehaven, where he continued for almost three years. For when the matter was discovered, his mother sent orders by all means not to hazard a second voyage, till he could be better able to bear it. The nurse was so careful of him that before he returned he had learnt to spell; and by the time that he was five years old he could read any chapter in the Bible.

After his return to Ireland, he was sent at six years old to the school of Kilkenny, from whence, at fourteen, he was admitted into the university at Dublin; where, by the ill-treatment of his nearest relations, he was so much discouraged and sunk in his spirits that he too much neglected some parts of his academic studies, for which he had no great relish by nature, and turned himself to reading history and poetry ...

Verses Wrote in a Lady's Ivory Table-Book

Anglo-Irish statesman, writer and thinker Sir William Temple was a lasting influence on Swift, who later was to edit his papers for publication. He worked as Temple's secretary, and his duties included tutoring the housekeeper's small daughter, Esther Johnson. Temple introduced his employee to many of England's great and good, and soon this entertaining and ambitious Irishman was being invited to stay in places like Berkeley Castle, and discovering other haunts of the political elite.

In these lines, from 1698 or so, Swift gleefully contrasts the conventional falsities of courtship in these houses with the banal daily concerns of a young lady who needs to attract a rich beau to marry. An ivory table-book was a combined visitor's book and luxury jotter, in which entries could be rubbed out and written over.

Peruse my leaves through every part,

And think thou seest my owner's heart;

Scrawled o'er with trifles thus; and quite

As hard, as senseless, and as light:

Exposed to every coxcomb's eyes,   [fop's

But hid with caution from the wise.

Here may you read, 'Dear charming saint',

Beneath 'A new receipt for paint.'   [recipe for cosmetics

Here, in beau-spelling, 'Tru tel death,'

There, in her own, 'For an el breath.'   [halitosis

Here, 'Lovely nymph pronounce my doom,'

There, 'A safe way to use perfume.'

Here, a page filled with billets-doux; [messages of love

On t'other side, 'Laid out for shoes.   [money spent on

(Madam, I die without your Grace.)

Item, for half a yard of lace.'

Who that had wit would place it here,

For every peeping fop to jeer?

To think that your brain's issue is   [that your thoughts are

Exposed to th'excrement of his,

In power of spittle and a clout,   [a cloth

Whene'er he please, to blot it out;

And then to heighten the disgrace,

Clap his own nonsense in the place.

Whoe'er expects to hold his part

In such a book, and such a heart,

If he be wealthy, and a fool,

Is in all points the fittest tool;

Of whom it may be justly said,

He's a gold pencil tipped with lead.

From A LETTER TO STELLA AND HER MOTHER

Sent in early 1698, this is the first letter from Swift to Esther Johnson ('Stella') to have survived. It may even be the first he ever wrote to her. He is thirty, she seventeen. With her mother and Sir William, she has gone for a season to Temple's London residence, while Swift is left behind to keep an eye on Moor Park.

I received your kind letter from Robert by word of mouth, and think it a vast condescension in you to think of us in all your greatness. Now shall we hear nothing from you for five months but 'we courtiers'. Loory [a bird of paradise] is well, and presents his humble duty to my lady, and love to his fellow servant: but he is the miserablest creature in the world; eternally in his melancholy note, whatever I can do ...

Nothing grows better by your absence but my lady's chamber floor, and Tumbledown Dick. Here are three letters for you, and Molly will not send one of them; she says you ordered her to the contrary. Mr Mose [Temple's steward] and I desire you will remember our love to the King [William III], and let us know how he looks.

Robert says the Czar [Peter the Great, then in London] is there, and is fallen in love with you, and designs to carry you to Muscovy [Moscow]; pray provide yourself with muffs and sable tippets, etc.

Aeolus [*i.e.* the wind] has made a strange revolution in the rooks' nests; but I say no more, for it is dangerous to meddle with things above us.

I desire your absence heartily, for now I live in great state, and the cook comes in to know what I please to have for dinner: I ask very gravely what is in the house, and accordingly give orders for a dish of pigeons, or, etc. You shall have no more ale here, unless you send us a letter. Here is a great bundle and a letter for you; both came together from London. We all keep home like so many cats ...

A MEDITATION UPON A BROOMSTICK

Staying at Berkeley Castle in 1701, Swift had to read aloud to the Earl's wife. One of her favourite books was *Occasional Reflections on Several Subjects* – saccharine, sermon-like musings by the Irish chemist Robert Boyle. Swift wrote a Reflection of his own, laced with half-concealed bawdiness, and slipped it into the book. When he read out the title, Lady Berkeley exclaimed, 'Bless me, what a strange subject! But there is no knowing what useful lessons of instruction this wonderful man may draw from things apparently the most trivial.' Afterwards, when the spoof was discovered: 'What a vile trick has that rogue played me! But it is his way ...' Swift was not asked to read any more from the tedious book.

This single stick, which you now behold ingloriously lying in that neglected corner, I once knew in a flourishing state in a forest: it was full of sap, full of leaves, and full of boughs: but now, in vain does the busy art of man pretend to vie with nature, by tying that withered bundle of twigs to its sapless trunk: it is now, at best, but the reverse of what it was, a tree turned upside down, the branches on the earth, and the root in the air; it is now handled by every dirty wench, condemned to do her drudgery, and, by a capricious kind of fate, destined to make other things clean, and be nasty itself: at length, worn to the stumps in the service of the maids, it is either thrown out of doors, or condemned to its last use, of kindling a fire.

When I beheld this, I sighed, and said within myself, *Surely mortal man is a broomstick!* Nature sent him into the world strong and lusty, in a thriving condition, wearing his own hair on his head, the proper branches of this reasoning vegetable, until the axe of intemperance has lopped off his green boughs and left him a withered trunk: he then flies to art, and puts on a periwig, valuing himself upon an unnatural bundle of hairs (all covered with powder), that never grew on his head; but now, should this our broomstick pretend to enter the scene, proud of those birchen spoils it never bore, and all covered with dust, though the sweepings of the finest lady's chamber, we should be apt to ridicule and despise its vanity, partial judges that we are of our own excellencies and other men's defaults.

But a broomstick, perhaps, you will say, is an emblem of a tree standing on its head. And pray, what is man, but a topsy-turvy creature, his animal faculties perpetually mounted on his rational, his head where his heels should be, grovelling on the earth? And yet with all his faults, he sets up to be a universal reformer and corrector of abuses, a remover of grievances; rakes into every slut's corner of nature, bringing hidden corruption to the light; and raises a mighty dust where there was none before, sharing deeply all the while in the very same pollutions he pretends to sweep away.

His laſt days are ſpent in slavery to women, and generally the leaſt deserving, till, worn out to the ſtumps, like his brother besom, he is either kicked out of doors, or made use of to kindle flames for others to warm themselves by.

From MRS FRANCES HARRIS'S PETITION TO THEIR EXCELLENCIES THE LORDS JUSTICES OF IRELAND

This dramatic glimpse of life below ſtairs in Berkeley Caſtle in 1701 is a sort of rap, an outpouring of complaints and explanations by the Countess's waiting-maid, who has mislaid some money. All his life, Swift liſtened to and talked with ordinary people – the poor and the wronged – with as much intereſt as he paid to those at the far end of the social scale.

THE HUMBLE PETITION of Frances Harris,
Who muſt ſtarve, and die a maid if it miscarries
Humbly sheweth, that I went to warm myself in Lady Betty's
    chamber, because I was cold,
And I had in a purse seven pound, four shillings, and six-
    pence (besides farthings), in money and gold;

So because I had been buying things for my Lady laſt night,
I was resolved to tell my money, to see if ît was right. [to count
     Now, you muſt know, because my trunk has a very bad lock,
     Therefore all the money I have (which, God knows, is a very
     small ſtock)
     I keep in my pocket tied about my middle, next my smock.
So when I went to put up my purse, as God would have ît, my
     smock was unrîpped
And inſtead of putting ît into my pocket, down ît slîpped;
Then the bell rung, and I went down to put my Lady to bed,
And, God knows, I thought my money was as safe as my maid-
     enhead.
So, when I came up again, I found my pocket feel very light,
But when I searched, and missed my purse, Lord! I thought I
     should have sunk outright.

'Lord! Madam,' says Mary, 'how d'ye do?' 'Indeed,' said I,
     'never worse;
But pray, Mary, can you tell what I have done with my purse?'
'Lord help me!' says Mary, 'I never ſtirred out of this place!'
'Nay,' said I, 'I had ît in Lady Betty's chamber, that's a plain case.'
So Mary got me to bed, and covered me up warm:
However, she ſtole away my garters, that I might do myself no
     harm.

So I tumbled and tossed all night, as you may very well think,

But hardly ever set my eyes together, or slept a wink.

So I was a-dreamed, methought, that I went and searched the
folks round,

And in a corner of Mrs Dukes' box, tied in a rag, the money
was found.   [a footman's wife

So next morning we told Whittle, and he fell a-swearing;

[the Earl's valet

Then my dame Wadgar came, and she, you know, is thick of
hearing.   [the housekeeper

'Dame,' said I, as loud as I could bawl, 'do you know what a
loss I have had?'

'Nay,' says she, 'my Lord Collway's folks are all very sad,

[*i.e.* Galway

For my Lord Dromedary comes a Tuesday without fail.'

[*i.e.* Drogheda

'Pugh!' said I, 'but that's not the business that I ail.'

Says Cary, says he, 'I have been a servant this five and twenty
years come spring,   [clerk of the kitchen

And in all the places I lived, I never heard of such a thing.'

'Yes,' says the steward, 'I remember when I was at my Lady
Shrewsbury's,

Such a thing as this happened, just about the time of goose-
berries.' ...

From A TALE OF A TUB

In 1695, Swift was ordained, and went to be rector of
Kilroot, a parish in rural Ulster. Lonely and isolated among
rustics and Presbyterians, he returned to Moor Park as soon
as he could. After Temple's death in 1699, he was appointed
vicar of Laracor, near Trim, County Meath. He was to retain
the parish (which in reality would be run by various curates)
until his death, forty-six years later. When he could, he
went there to relax, planting willows and fruit trees, fishing
for trout and pike and, occasionally, preaching to the tiny
congregation. Then, in 1704, the Church of Ireland sent
him to intercede with Queen Anne on a matter of Church
taxes. Though the mission proved fruitless, he would be
based in London for the next decade.

1704 was also the year in which Swift's first major prose
work, *A Tale of a Tub,* appeared. 'What a genius I had when I
wrote that book,' he remarked in old age, and indeed it is an
extraordinary performance. With statements like 'Last week
I saw a woman flayed, and you will hardly believe how much it
altered her person for the worse', very little in this complex,
many-sided satire can be taken purely at face value: anything
praised by the 'author' is likely to have been disliked by
Swift. The *Tale* is unlike any book written previously, for it is
a parody of the very nature of a book itself: in fact, the story

proper does not even begin until a third of the way through, since there are so many hypertextual forewords, dedications and introductions.

This short extract is a preposterous list of learned essays. It may owe something to the papers that Swift as a student would have heard in Dublin at the Philosophical Society.

Treatises written by the same author:

A Character of the present Set of Wits in this Island.

A panegyrical Essay upon the Number Three.

A Dissertation upon the principal Productions of Grub Street.

Lectures upon a Dissection of Human Nature.

A Panegyric upon the World.

An analytical Discourse upon Zeal, *histori-theo-physiologically* considered.

A general History of Ears.

A modest Defence of the Proceedings of the Rabble in all ages.

A Description of the Kingdom of Absurdities.

A Voyage into England, by a Person of Quality in *Terra Australis Incognita*, translated from the Original.

A critical Essay upon the Art of Canting [jargon], philosophically, physically, and musically considered.

J.S. Müller inv: del: et Sc:

Part the Second:

WELL, AYE, THE PAMPHLET.

BEING

a Selection of

VERSE & PROSE

from the **P**en of

Dr. Jonathan Swift

while residing in

the CITY of LONDON,

during the Opening Years

of the

18th CENTURY.

A Description of the Morning

Stella, accompanied by her lifelong companion Mrs Dingley, had moved to Ireland in the early 1700s to be with Swift, only to find that he was spending most of his time in London, writing and advising politicians. This mock-pastoral poem appeared in the *Tatler* in 1709. Instead of idealised rural imagery, Swift drew on what he saw going on around his lodgings in the West End. Injustice runs through the life of the city, where children are sent up chimneys, women are drunk, mad or desperate, and jailors let prisoners out at night to steal for them. The citizens are often up to no good — a servant has been sleeping with her boss, employees pretend to be working, the upper classes don't paid their bills. Despite everything, the poem seems to invite empathy with these people, leaving us with the universal picture of little boys who are in no rush at all to get to school.

Now hardly here and there an hackney-coach
Appearing, showed the ruddy morn's approach.
Now Betty from her master's bed had flown,
And softly stole to discompose her own;
The slip-shod 'prentice from his master's door

Had pared the dirt, and sprinkled round the floor.
Now Moll had whirled her mop with dexterous airs,
Prepared to scrub the entry and the stairs.
The youth with broomy stumps began to trace
The kennel's edge, where wheels had worn the place.
[the gutter, to find old nails (Swift's note)
The small-coal man was heard with cadence deep,
Till drowned in shriller notes of chimney-sweep:
Duns at his lordship's gate began to meet;   [debt collectors
And brickdust Moll had screamed through half the street.
The turnkey now his flock returning sees,   [jailor
Duly let out a-nights to steal for fees:
The watchful bailiffs take their silent stands,
And schoolboys lag with satchels in their hands.

From A DESCRIPTION OF A CITY SHOWER

More mop-whirling in another 'pastoral' from the *Tatler*, full
of London citizens and cleansing rain. Modelled on Virgil's
Georgics, it was one of Swift's own favourites. Soon after it
was published in October 1710, he wrote to Stella and Mrs
Dingley: 'They say 'tis the best thing I ever writ, and I think
so too. I suppose the Bishop of Clogher will show it you.

Pray tell me how you like ît.' No satisfactory reply can have reached him from Ireland, for a month later, he told the ladies that the bishop had informed him by letter that 'you both swore ît was *Shaver*, and not *Shower*. You all lie, and you are puppies ...'

Careful observers may foretell the hour
(By sure prognoſtics) when to dread a shower.
While rain depends, the pensive cat gives o'er   [threatens
Her frolics, and pursues her tail no more.
Returning home at night, you find the sink   [sewer
Strike your offended sense wîth double ſtink.
If you be wise, then go not far to dine:
You ſpend in coach-hire more than save in wine ...
Meanwhile the south, rising wîth dabbled wings,
A sable cloud athwart the welkin flings,   [across the skies
That swilled more liquor than ît could contain,
And, like a drunkard, gives ît up again.
Brisk Susan whîps her linen from the rope,
While the firſt drizzling shower is borne aslope;
Such is that ſprinkling which some careless quean   [slattern
Flirts on you from her mop, but not so clean:
You fly, invoke the gods; then, turning, ſtop
To rail; she singing, ſtill whirls on her mop ...

Now in contiguous drops the flood comes down,

Threatening with deluge this devoted town.

To shops in crowds the daggled females fly,   [splattered

Pretend to cheapen goods, but nothing buy.   [bargain for

The Templar spruce, while every spout's abroach,

                                                    [young lawyer; gushing

Stays till 'tis fair, yet seems to call a coach.

The tucked-up seamstress walks with hasty strides,

While streams run down her oiled umbrella's sides.

Here various kinds, by various fortunes led,

Commence acquaintance underneath a shed.

Triumphant Tories, and desponding Whigs

Forget their feuds, and join to save their wigs ...

Now from all parts the swelling kennels flow,   [gutters

And bear their trophies with them as they go:

Filth of all hues and odours seems to tell

What streets they sailed from, by their sight and smell.

They, as each torrent drives with rapid force,

From Smithfield to St Pulchre's shape their course,

                                    [St Sepulchre's Church, Holborn

And in huge confluence joined at Snow Hill ridge,

Fall from the conduit prone to Holborn Bridge.

Sweeping from butchers' stalls, dung, guts, and blood,

Drowned puppies, stinking sprats, all drenched in mud,

Dead cats, and turnip-tops, come tumbling down the flood.

From JOURNAL TO STELLA
LETTER XXXVIII, 8 JANUARY 1712

When apart, Swift and Stella corresponded incessantly. His surviving letters reveal a love that, while intense, seems paternal rather than amorous. He normally wrote to Stella and Mrs Dingley from his bed, often using his 'little language' — a sort of nursery talk, in which he was 'Pdfr' or 'Podefar' and the ladies 'MD'. From 1710 to 1713, these gossipy, affectionate letters chronicle his life, from political wheeler-dealing and his latest pamphlets and poems, to his private affairs — though he does not mention everything, and particularly avoids talking about his neighbour, Miss Vanhomrig ('Vanessa'), a beautiful Irish girl with whom he drinks a great deal of coffee. Notable, however, are Swift's nostalgic mentions of the Parish of Laracor, where, in the early days of the century, he and Stella (and of course Mrs D.) had spent many happy days: the ladies had taken a cottage nearby. It's a pity that Stella's side of the long exchange has not survived, but her tone can be gathered from Swift's replies (which were later published as *Journal to Stella*). The following passage has been extracted almost at random:

8th January. Well then, come, let us see this letter; if I muſt answer ît, I muſt. What's here now? Yes, faîth, I lamented my birthday two days after, and that's all: and you rhyme, Madam Stella; were those verses made upon my birthday? Faîth, when I read them, I had them running in my head all the day, and said them over a thousand times; they drank your health in all their glasses, and wished, etc. I could not get them out of my head …

Stella is a good ĝirl for not being angry when I tell her of ſpelling; I see none wrong in this. God Almighty be praised that your disorders lessen; ît increases my hopes mightily that they will go off. And have you been plagued wîth the fear of the plague? Never mind those reports; I have heard them five hundred times … I ſtated Dingley's accounts in my laſt. I forgot Catherine's sevenpenny dinner. I hope ît was the beef-ſteaks; I'll call and eat them in Spring; but Goody Stoyte muſt ĝive me coffee, or green tea, for I drink no bohea. Well, aye, the pamphlet; but there are some addîtions to the fourth edîtion; the fifth edîtion was of four thousand, in a smaller print, sold for sixpence … Pray now eat the Laracor apples; I beg you not to keep them, but tell me what they are. You have had Tooke's bill in my laſt. And so there now, your whole letter is answered. I tell you what I do; I lay your letter before me, and take ît in order, and answer what is necessary; and so and so … 9th January. I could not go sleep laſt night till paſt two, and was waked before three by a noise of people endeavouring

to break open my window. For a while I would not stir, thinking it might be my imagination; but hearing the noise continued, I rose and went to the window, and then it ceased. I went to bed again, and heard it repeated more violently; then I rose and called up the house, and got a candle: the rogues had lifted up the sash a yard; there are great sheds before my windows, although my lodgings be a storey high; and if they get upon the sheds they are almost even with my window. We observed their track, and panes of glass fresh broken. The watchmen told us today they saw them, but could not catch them. They attacked others in the neighbourhood about the same time, and actually robbed a house in Suffolk Street, which is the next street but one to us. It is said they are seamen discharged from service. I went up to call my man, and found his bed empty; it seems he often lies abroad. I challenged him this morning as one of the robbers. He is a sad dog; and the minute I come to Ireland I will discard him. I have this day got double iron bars to every window in my dining-room and bed-chamber; and I hide my purse in my thread stocking between the bed's head and the wainscot ...

Epigram

We muſt not be tempted to read this cynical tale from 1712 as a glimpse of Swift's opinion of the perils of marriage. It was collećted by Stella in a transcrîption she made of all the verses by him that she could find.

As Thomas was cudgelled one day by his wife,
He took to the ſtreet, and fled for his life:
Tom's three deareſt friends came by in the squabble,
And saved him at once from the shrew and the rabble;
Then ventured to ǵive him some sober advice —
But Tom is a person of honour so nice,
Too wise to take counsel, too proud to take warning,
That he sent to all three a challenge next morning:
Three duels he fought, thrice ventured his life;
Went home, and was cudgelled again by his wife

From THE AUTHOR UPON HIMSELF

By 1714, Swift's time in London was coming to an end. His influence in the moſt exalted polîtical circles as lobbyiſt/consultant had led inevîtably to resentment from rivals and opponents wîth the ear of Queen Anne. At one point he narrowly escaped imprisonment when it was hinted that he supported the royal claims of the 'Old Pretender', James Stuart, son of James II. In these lines, Swift may for once be speaking from the heart: though the poem has an ironic twinkle in its eye, it addresses itself directly to the reader, without satire. It would not be published until after his death.

… Swift had the sin of wit, no venial crime;
Nay, 'twas affirmed, he sometimes dealt in rhyme;
Humour and mirth had place in all he writ;
He reconciled divinity and wit:
He moved and bowed, and talked with too much grace,
Nor showed the parson in his gait or face;
Despised luxurious wines and costly meat,
Yet still was at the tables of the great …
But, after sage monitions from his friends,   [warnings
His talents to employ for nobler ends,
To better judgments willing to submit,
He turns to politics his dangerous wit.

And now, the public interest to support,
By Harley Swift invited, comes to court;   [Lord Treasurer
In favour grows with ministers of state;
Admitted private, when superiors wait:

And Harley, not ashamed his choice to own,   [to admit
Takes him to Windsor in his coach alone ...

Now Finch alarms the Lords: he hears for certain

                                              [Earl of Nottingham
This dangerous priest is got behind the curtain: ...
'A certain doctor is observed of late   [*i.e.* Dr Swift
To haunt a certain minister of state:
From whence with half an eye we may discover
The peace is made, and Perkin must come over.'

                                              [nickname of the 'Pretender'
York is from Lambeth sent, to show the queen
A dangerous treatise writ against the spleen;   [*i.e. A Tale of a Tub*
Which, by the style, the matter, and the drift,
'Tis thought could be the work of none but Swift ...

Now through the realm a proclamation spread,
To fix a price on his devoted head ...

By faction tired, with grief he waits awhile,
His great contending friends to reconcile;
Performs what friendship, justice, truth require:
What could he more, but decently retire?

I.S.Müller inv: del et Sc:

Part the Third:

MY SMALL DOMINIONS.

BEING

A

Selection of

COMPOSITIONS,

in Verse & in Prose,

from the Pen of

the Very Reverend Doctor Swift,

writ while he was

Dean

of St Patrick's Cathedral,

Dublin, Ireland.

The Author's Manner of Living

Now in Dublin as Dean of St Patrick's Cathedral, though the job was as important as a bishopric would have been, Swift felt he had been outflanked by political enemies who wanted him out of the way. He was often at loggerheads with the Irish Bench of Bishops. In 1719, he suggested that all the new ones were really highwaymen, who had murdered the real appointees on Hounslow Heath and stolen their episcopal robes. He missed life in London, and the gatherings with other poets and writers at the Scriblerus Club in St James's Palace. He wrote at around this time to Alexander Pope:

'You are to understand that I live in the corner of a vast unfurnished house. My family consists of a steward, a groom, a helper in the stable, a footman, and an old maid, who are all at board wages, and when I do not dine abroad, or make an entertainment, which last is very rare, I eat a mutton-pie, and drink half a pint of wine. My amusements are defending my small dominions against the Archbishop, and endeavouring to reduce my rebellious choir. *Perditur haec inter misero lux.* ['Amid such matters, the day is wasted.' (Horace)] I desire you will present my humble service to Mr Addison, Mr Congreve, and Mr Rowe, and Gay ...'

On rainy days alone I dine,

Upon a chick and pint of wine.

On rainy days I dine alone,

And pick my chicken to the bone;

But this my servants much enrages:

No scraps remain to save board-wages.

                             [their allowance for living expenses

In weather fine I nothing spend,

But often sponge upon a friend;

Yet, where he's not so rich as I,

I pay my club, and so goodbye.   [pay my share

From ON SLEEPING IN CHURCH: A SERMON

The Dean of St Patrick's Cathedral didn't think much of his own sermons, calling them 'preaching pamphlets', and most of them have been lost, including a batch of thirty passed on to his friend, the schoolmaster Thomas Sheridan, when he took holy orders. In this one, having observed that 'opium is not so stupefying to many persons as an afternoon sermon,' he draws a moral from the inattention of his flock. The sermon begins:

In the ninth verse of the twentieth chapter of the Acts of the Apostles it is written:

And there sat in the window a certain young man, named Eutychus, being fallen into a deep sleep; and while Paul was long preaching, he sunk down with sleep, and fell down from the third loft, and was taken up dead.

I have chosen these words with design, if possible, to disturb some part in this audience of half an hour's sleep, for the convenience and exercise whereof this place, at this season of the day, is very much celebrated.

There is indeed one mortal disadvantage to which all preaching is subject; that those who, by the wickedness of their lives, stand in greatest need, have usually the smallest share; for either they are absent upon the account of idleness, or spleen, or hatred to religion, or in order to doze away the intemperance of the week: or, if they do come, they are sure to employ their minds rather any other way than regarding or attending to the business of the place.

The accident which happened to this young man in the text, hath not been sufficient to discourage his successors: but, because the preachers now in the world, however they may exceed St Paul in the art of setting men to sleep, do extremely fall short of him in the working of miracles; therefore men are become so cautious, as to choose more safe and convenient stations and postures for taking their repose, without hazard of their persons ...

Swift, the deaf preaching to the deaf, ends his sermon resoundingly:

> *He that hath ears to hear, let him hear.* And God give us all grace to hear and receive His holy word to the salvation of our own souls!

From PHYLLIS, OR THE PROGRESS OF LOVE

The dangers of a hasty marriage: one of Swift's most popular comic verses. Thought to have been written in 1719, it charts the downfall of a highly respectable young lady.

Desponding Phyllis was endued
With every talent of a prude:
She trembled when a man drew near;
Salute her, and she turned her ear:
If o'er against her you were placed,
She durst not look above your waist:
She'd rather take you to her bed
Than let you see her dress her head;
In church you hear her, through the crowd,
Repeat the absolution loud;
In church, secure behind her fan,

She durst behold that monster, man;
There practised how to place her head,
And bit her lips to make them red;
Or, on the mat devoutly kneeling,
Would lift her eyes up to the ceiling,
And heave her bosom, unaware,
For neighbouring beaux to see it bare.

At length a lucky lover came,
And found admittance to the dame,
Suppose all parties now agreed,
The writings drawn, the lawyer fee'd,
The vicar and the ring bespoke:
Guess, how could such a match be broke?
See then what mortals place their bliss in!
Next morn betimes the bride was missing.
The mother screamed, the father chid: [chided, nagged
Where can this idle wretch be hid?
No news of Phyl! The bridegroom came,
And thought his bride had skulked for shame,
Because her father used to say
The girl had such a bashful way.

Now John the butler must be sent
To learn the road that Phyllis went:

The groom was wished to saddle Crop,   [a family horse
For John must neither light nor stop,   [alight
But find her wheresoe'er she fled,
And bring her back, alive or dead.

See here again the devil to do!
For truly John was missing too:
The horse and pillion both were gone!
Phyllis, it seems, was fled with John ...

Fair maidens all, attend the Muse,
Who now the wandering pair pursues:
Away they rode in homely sort,
Their journey long, their money short;
The loving couple well bemired;
The horse and both the riders tired;
Their victuals bad, their lodgings worse;
Phyl cried, and John began to curse;
Phyl wished that she had strained a limb
When first she ventured out with him;
John wished that he had broke a leg,
When first for her he quitted Peg.

But what adventures more befell 'em,
The Muse hath now no time to tell 'em;

How Johnny wheedled, threatened, fawned,

Till Phyllis all her trinkets pawned:

How oft she broke her marriage vows,

In kindness to maintain her spouse,

Till swains unwholesome spoiled the trade;

For now the surgeon must be paid,

To whom those perquisites are gone,   [privileges

In Christian justice due to John.

When food and raiment now grew scarce,

Fate put a period to the farce,

And with exact poetic justice;

For John was landlord, Phyllis hostess:

They keep, at Staines, the Old Blue Boar,

Are cat and dog, and rogue and whore.

From THE DESCRIPTION OF AN IRISH FEAST

TRANSLATED ALMOST LITERALLY OUT OF THE ORIGINAL IRISH

This lively song from 1720 was set to music by the harper Turlough O Carolan, who is likely to have known the Dean. It describes a celebration held by an Ulster chieftain before he sets off to visit the court of Queen Elizabeth. A rare link between Swift and the Gaelic tradition: though interested in Hibernian speech patterns and idioms, he probably never learned much Irish, and fashioned these verses from a supplied prose translation.

O'Rourk's noble fare
Will ne'er be forgot,
By those who were there,
Or those who were not.

His revels to keep,
We sup and we dine
On seven score sheep,
Fat bullocks, and swine.

Usquebagh to our feast   [whiskey
In pails was brought up,
A hundred at least,
And a madder our cup.   [square wooden bowl

O there is the sport,
We rise with the light
In disorderly sort,
From snoring all night ...

Come, harper, strike up,
But first, by your favour,
Boy, give us a cup;
Ay, this hath some savour:

O'Rourk's jolly boys
Ne'er dreamt of the matter,
Till, roused by the noise,
And musical clatter,

They bounce from their nest,
No longer will tarry,
They rise ready dressed,
Without one *Ave Mary.*

They dance in a round,
Cutting capers and ramping;   [romping
A mercy the ground
Did not burst with their stamping.

The floor is all wet
With leaps and with jumps,
While the water and sweat
Splish-splash in their pumps ...

Good Lord, what a sight,
After all their good cheer,
For people to fight
In the midst of their beer:

They rise from their feast,
And hot are their brains,
A cubit at least   [about 18 inches
The length of their skeans.   [knives, daggers

What stabs and what cuts,
What clattering of sticks;
What strokes on the guts,
What bastings and kicks!

With cudgels of oak,
Well hardened in flame,
An hundred heads broke,
An hundred struck lame ...

Come down with that beam,
If cudgels are scarce,
A blow on the weam,   [belly
Or a kick on the arse.

FISH ON FRIDAY

Periodically, Swift went off on expeditions, travelling through Ireland on horseback, calling on friends and chatting to whoever he happened to meet along the way. Reports of his adventures and encounters on these trips have come down to us, largely through the oral storytelling tradition. Interesting as they are, few of these tales can be relied upon – one story, for example, features an adulterous Dean Swift's scolding wife – but others, it might be argued, have the ring of truth. This is said to have been Swift's reaction in a roadside tavern in Sixmilebridge, County Clare, when he was refused meat because it was the Roman Catholic 'fish' day:

Can any man of common sense
Think eating meat gives God offence
Or that the herring has a charm
The Almighty's anger to disarm?
Wrapped up in majesty divine,
Does He reflect on what we dine?

J. S. Müller inv del et Sc:

Part the Fourth:

THE DANGER OF A FRIEND.

BEING

A

Gathering of

VERSES

&

EXCURSIONS IN PROSE

from the pen & heart of

"PODEFAR,"

personal Sobriquet

of

J. Swift, D.S.P.C.

Stella's Birthday (1719)

Stella, ever since her childhood years in Moor Park, had been an indispensable element of Swift's inner life. Now she often played a part as hostess in the Deanery, and usually lived there (with Mrs Dingley) when he was away. There is good evidence that they were secretly married in 1716, but there is also good evidence that they weren't. To confuse matters, Esther Vanhomrig ('Vanessa') had fallen in love with Swift in London, and in 1714 had followed him to Ireland, with marriage in mind. For seven years, they met frequently — alone — in her Dublin house. The long poem 'Cadenus and Vanessa', which he wrote in her honour, ominously included the lines, referring to himself (Cadenus), 'He now could praise, esteem, approve, / But understood not what was love.' Eventually he was urging her to go, to leave Ireland, firmly telling her so in a letter in 1721 — before signing off with the words (in French), 'Be assured that apart from you, nobody has ever been loved, honoured, esteemed, adored by your friend.'

What happened between Vanessa and the Dean was the stuff of frenzied gossip and speculation, both at the time and long after their deaths; it is now an insoluble mystery. Vanessa never went away. She died in 1723, not long after Swift seems finally to have broken with her. One hypothesis goes that they had had a son together, who after Vanessa's death was brought up by Stella under the name of Bryan M'Loghlin, but that he too died, and was buried in St Patrick's Cathedral in 1731. Another theory suggests that Stella and Swift had the same father, Sir William Temple. It may be enough to say that Swift's deepest loyalty always lay with Stella, even though, as seems likely, the bond between them was not a sexual one.

With the benign humour that was generally part of their rapport, the Dean wrote this poem in 1719 to celebrate Stella's thirty-eighth birthday. Though she was only eight when he arrived at Wood Park, here he remembers her as she was at sixteen, and (perhaps reflecting a certain ambivalence in their relationship) he conjures up a universe in which there could be two Stellas, with two Swifts to woo them.

Stella this day is thirty-four
(We shan't dispute a year or more);
However, Stella, be not troubled,
Although thy size and years are doubled,
Since first I saw thee at sixteen,
The brightest virgin on the green.
So little is thy form declined
Made up so largely in thy mind.

Oh, would it please the gods to split
Thy beauty, size, and years, and wit,
No age could furnish out a pair
Of nymphs so graceful, wise and fair:
With half the lustre of your eyes,
With half your wit, and years, and size:
And then before it grew too late,
How should I beg of gentle fate
(That either nymph might have her swain)
To split my worship too in twain.

From STELLA AT WOOD PARK, A HOUSE OF CHARLES FORD, ESQ., NEAR DUBLIN

This is one of Swift's most entertaining and revealing poems about Stella. By 1723, her weight, having gone up, was going down again. Swift was worried, with reason, about her physical health – and perhaps about her mental health too. Immediately after the death of Vanessa, he asked Charles Ford ('Don Carlos'), a rich Irishman and a close friend in London, to allow her to stay with him – without Mrs Dingley for once – in his house in County Meath. By all reports, she appreciated the break. Swift went away too,

on a long trip out of the city, and remained out of touch for
months as he rode around Ireland. He wrote this later in
the year, when everything and everyone were back, more or
less, to normal.

Don Carlos, in a merry spite,
Did Stella to his house invite:
He entertained her half a year
With generous wines and costly cheer ...
Now at the table head she sits,
Presented with the nicest bits: ...
Don Carlos earnestly would beg,
'Dear Madam, try this pigeon's leg;' ...
Through candle-light she viewed the wine,
To see that every glass was fine.
At last, grown prouder than the devil
With feeding high, and treatment civil,
Don Carlos now began to find
His malice work as he designed.   [evil scheme
The winter sky began to frown:
Poor Stella must pack off to town;
From purling streams and fountains bubbling,
To Liffey's stinking tide in Dublin:
From wholesome exercise and air

To sossing in an easy-chair: [lounging

From ſtomach sharp, and hearty feeding,

To piddle like a lady breeding: [to pick at food as if pregnant

From ruling there the household singly.

To be directed here by Dingley:

From every day a lordly banquet,

To half a joint, and God be thank ît: ...

From Ford attending at her call,

To visîts of Archdeacon Wall: [Thomas Walls, a friend

From Ford, who thinks of nothing mean,   [niggardly

To the poor doings of the Dean ...

But now arrives the dismal day;

She muſt return to Ormonde Quay ...

Began a thousand faults to ſpy;

The ceiling hardly six feet high;

The smutty wainscot full of cracks:

And half the chairs wîth broken backs ...

Howe'er, to keep her ſpirîts up,

She sent for company to sup:

When all the while you might remark,

She ſtrove in vain to ape Wood Park.

Two bottles called for (half her ſtore,

The cupboard could contain but four);

A supper worthy of herself,

Five nothings in five plates of delf.

Thus for a week the farce went on;

When, all her country savings gone,

She fell into her former scene,

Small beer, a herring, and the Dean.

Thus far in jest: though now, I fear,

You think my jesting too severe; ...

I must confess your wine and vittle

I was too hard upon a little:

Your table neat, your linen fine;

And, though in miniature, you shine:

Yet, when you sigh to leave Wood Park,

The scene, the welcome, and the spark,   [the beau – *i.e.* Ford

To languish in this odious town,

And pull your haughty stomach down,   [grand airs

We think you quite mistake the case,

The virtue lies not in the place:

For though my raillery were true,

A cottage is Wood Park with you.

From THE BLUNDERS, DEFICIENCIES, DISTRESSES, AND MISFORTUNES OF QUILCA

One of Swift's closest male friends in Ireland was the schoolmaster Thomas Sheridan. He, or rather his formidable wife, owned a house in the muddy townland of Quilca, County Cavan. Swift first stayed there in October 1722, while he was writing *Gulliver's Travels*. (More folklore: a contributory spark for that book was said to be a local giant, Big Doughty, who impressed Swift one day by carrying a young horse over a fence.)

In April 1725, the Dean was back in Cavan, and this time, the Sheridans being away, he brought the rest of his entourage with him. He hoped that the country air would be good for Mrs Johnson (Stella). He wrote letters to friends, telling them about hiking with Stella over mountains and through bogs, and how she, with the little axe she carried at her waist, helped him 'levelling mountains and raising stones, and fencing against inconveniencies of a scanty lodging, want of victual, and a thieving race of people'. They would all be there for almost six months. The place had a few disadvantages, however – among other problems in the long, low, thatched cottage they found, according to Swift:

* The empty bottles all uncleanable.

* The vessels for drink few and leaky.

* One hinge of the ſtreet door broke off, and the people
    forced to go out and come in at the back door.

* The door of the Dean's bedchamber full of large chinks.

* The Dean's bed threatening every night to fall under him.

* The passages open overhead, by which the cats pass contin-
    ually into the cellar and eat the viſtuals, for which one was
    tried, condemned, and executed by the sword.

* The kitchen perpetually crowded with savages.

* Not a bit of mutton to be had in the country.

* Not a bit of turf this cold weather, and Mrs Johnson and the
    Dean in person, with all their servants, forced to assiſt at
    the bog in gathering up the wet bottoms of old clamps
    [piles of turf].

* The grate in the Ladies' bedchamber broke, and forced to
    be removed, by which they were compelled to be without
    fire, the chimney smoking intolerably, and the Dean's
    greatcoat was employed to ſtop the wind from coming
    down the chimney, without which expedient they muſt have
    been ſtarved [frozen] to death.

* The ſpit blunted with poking into bogs for timber, and tears
    the meat to pieces.

* A great hole in the floor of the Ladies' chamber, every hour
    hazarding a broken leg.

* The Ladies' and Dean's servants growing fast into the manners and thieveries of the natives; the Ladies themselves very much corrupted; the Dean perpetually storming, and in danger either of losing all his flesh, or sinking into barbarity for the sake of peace.

* Mrs Dingley full of cares for herself, and blunders and negligence for her friends. Mrs Johnson sick and helpless. The Dean deaf and fretting; the Lady's Maid awkward and clumsy; Robert lazy and forgetful; William a pragmatical, ignorant, and conceited puppy; Robin and Nurse the two great and only supports of the family.

* *Bellum lacteum:* Or, the milky battle, fought between the Dean and the crew of Quilca; the latter insisting on their privilege of not milking till eleven in the forenoon; whereas Mrs Johnson wanted milk at eight for her health. In this battle the Dean got the victory; but the crew of Quilca begin to rebel again, for it is this day almost ten o'clock, and Mrs Johnson hath not got her milk.

From STELLA'S BIRTHDAY (1927)

But though the fresh Cavan air seemed to have done Stella some good — the best medicine being, as Swift said elsewhere, 'Dr Diet, Dr Quiet and Dr Merriman' — it couldn't be denied that her health was inexorably going downhill. His last birthday poem to her reads more like a requiem than a celebration. He praises her stoicism, her charitable work and her care for him during an illness in 1724, when she had tended him 'like an humble slave'.

This day, whate'er the Fates decree,
Shall still be kept with joy by me:
This day then let us not be told,
That you are sick, and I grown old;
Nor think on our approaching ills,
And talk of spectacles and pills.
Tomorrow will be time enough
To hear such mortifying stuff ...

Although we now can form no more
Long schemes of life, as heretofore;
Yet you, while time is running fast,
Can look with joy on what is past ...

Say, Stella, feel you no content,
Reflecting on a life well spent?
Your skilful hand employed to save
Despairing wretches from the grave;

And then supporting with your store
Those whom you dragged from death before? ...

Believe me, Stella, when you show
That true contempt for things below,
Nor prize your life for other ends,
Than merely to oblige your friends;
Your former actions claim their part,
And join to fortify your heart.
For Virtue, in her daily race,
Like Janus, bears a double face;   [Roman god
Looks back with joy where she has gone
And therefore goes with courage on:
She at your sickly couch will wait,
And guide you to a better state.

O then, whatever Heaven intends,
Take pity on your pitying friends!
Nor let your ills affect your mind,
To fancy they can be unkind.
Me, surely me, you ought to spare,
Who gladly would your sufferings share;
Or give my scrap of life to you,
And think it far beneath your due;
You, to whose care so oft I owe
That I'm alive to tell you so.

HOLYHEAD, SEPTEMBER 25, 1727

In the summer of 1727, Swift was again in London, for what was to be the laſt time in his life. When Thomas Sheridan wrote to tell him that Stella was now very seriously ill, he thought at firſt of fleeing to Salisbury Plain or even to France, but in great diſtress finally decided to get the boat back to Ireland. He crossed England and Wales by coach to Holyhead, but there were no sailings to Dublin, and he had to waît there for almoſt a week, finally boarding a ſhîþ bound for County Down. To pass the time, he wrote a journal, which contained this cry of misery and fruſtration:

Lo here I ſît at Holyhead
Wîth muddy ale and mouldy bread:
All Chriſtian viĉtuals ſtink of fish,
I'm where my enemies would wish.
Conviĉt of lies is every sign: [guilty
The inn has not one drop of wine.
I'm faſtened both by wind and tide
I see the ſhîþ at anchor ride.
The Captain swears the sea's too rough
He has not passengers enough.

And thus the Dean is forced to ſtay

Till others come to help the pay.

In Dublin they'd be glad to see

A packet though ît brings in me.   [mailboat

They cannot say the winds are cross;

Your poliîticians at a loss

For want of matter swears and frets,

Are forced to read the old gazettes.

I never was in haſte before

To reach that slavish hateful shore:

Before, I always found the wind

To me was moſt malicious kind,

But now, the danger of a friend

On whom my fears and hopes depend,

Absent from whom all climes are cursed,

Wîth whom I'm happy in the worſt,

Wîth rage impatient makes me waît

A passage to the land I hate.

Else, rather on this bleaky shore

Where loudeſt winds incessant roar,

Where neîther herb nor tree will thrive,

Where nature hardly seems alive,

I'd go in freedom to my grave,

Than rule yon isle and be a slave.   [i.e., Ireland

From ON THE DEATH OF MRS JOHNSON

In fact, Stella would linger on for another four months, during which time she made her will (including a legacy to 'Bryan M'Loghlin, a child who now lives with me and whom I keep on charity'). Swift spent many hours at her bedside, watching and praying. When she died, he was not present, however, and he could not bring himself to officiate at – or even to attend – her funeral. Instead, he hid away in the Deanery, writing about her.

This day, being Sunday, January 28, 1728, about eight o'clock at night, a servant brought me a note, with an account of the death of the truest, most virtuous, and valuable friend, that I, or perhaps any other person, ever was blessed with ...

This is the night of the funeral, which my sickness will not suffer me to attend. It is now nine at night, and I am removed into another apartment, that I may not see the light in the church, which is just over against the window of my bed chamber ...

With all the softness of temper that became a lady, she had the personal courage of a hero. She and her friend having removed their lodgings to a new house, which stood solitary, a parcel of rogues, armed, attempted the house, where there was only one boy. She was then about four-and-twenty; and having been warned to apprehend some such attempt, she learned the management of a pistol; and the other women and servants being half dead with fear, she stole softly to her dining-room window, put on a black hood to prevent being seen, primed the pistol fresh, gently lifted up the sash, and taking her aim with the utmost presence of mind, discharged the pistol, loaden with the bullets, into the body of one villain, who stood the fairest mark. The fellow, mortally wounded, was carried off by the rest, and died the next morning; but his companions could not be found.

She loved Ireland much better than the generality of those who owe both their birth and riches to it; and left ... one thousand pounds to Dr Stephens' Hospital. She detested the tyranny and injustice of England, in their treatment of this kingdom. She had indeed reason to love a country, where she had the esteem and friendship of all who knew her, and the universal good report of all who ever heard of her ...

J.S. Müller inv. del. et Sc:

Part the Fifth:

LAUGHTER AND ADMIRATION.

BEING

A

Sampler of

PROVOCATIVE PASSAGES

From the BOOK entitled

TRAVELS

INTO SEVERAL

Remote NATIONS

of the

WORLD,

in Four Parts.

By

Lemuel GULLIVER,

First a Surgeon,

then a Captain of several Ships.

From GULLIVER'S TRAVELS

Swift's most famous book was an immediate success: everyone was reading it. Some people enjoyed it as a true account of a real man's adventures — just like *Robinson Crusoe* seven years earlier. Others were less sure: 'A bishop here,' Swift reported, 'said that book was full of improbable lies and for his part he hardly believed a word of it.' Most devoured it as the fantastic story it is. But some recognised that it was a devastating satire, and that it contained innumerable libellous criticisms of corruption in the Government, the Church and the Monarchy in England.

When the book was first published, both its author and its printer believed they were taking a serious risk. Swift went to great lengths to ensure that he could not be proved to have written it — though many people suspected he had. However, though it was widely criticised for coarseness, it was never prosecuted — primarily because, as he had once remarked (in *The Battle of the Books*), 'Satire is a sort of glass, wherein beholders do generally discover everybody's face but their own.'

Though today it is simply called *Gulliver's Travels*, the original title was *Travels into Several Remote Nations of the World*; its author was 'Lemuel Gulliver, first a Surgeon, and then a Captain of several Ships'. The book is divided into four voyages, on each of which the traveller discovers more about himself and about the nature and follies of mankind. On the final voyage, in the land of the Houyhnhnms, he encounters the loathsome Yahoos, feral human beings, but he lives with a race of rational horses. The Houyhnhnms are so principled and honourable that they do not understand even the concept of a lie. By the time he gets home at the end of the book, convinced that his fellow human beings are Yahoos — irretrievably vile, sordid, corrupt and wicked — Lemuel Gulliver is no longer sane.

Part I: A Voyage to Lilliput

I attempted to rise, but was not able to stir: for as I happened to lie on my back, I found my arms and legs were strongly fastened on each side to the ground; and my hair, which was long and thick, tied down in the same manner ... In a little time I felt something alive moving on my left leg, which advancing gently forward over my breast, came almost up to my chin; when, bending my eyes downwards as much as I could, I perceived it to be a human creature not six inches high, with a bow and arrow in his hands, and a quiver at his back. [Chapter 1]

The court was under many difficulties concerning me. They apprehended my breaking loose; that my diet would be very expensive, and might cause a famine. Sometimes they determined to starve me; or at least to shoot me in the face and hands with poisoned arrows, which would soon despatch me; but again they considered that the stench of so large a carcass might produce a plague in the metropolis, and probably spread through the whole kingdom. [Chapter 2]

[The emperor] desired I would stand like a Colossus, with my legs as far asunder as I conveniently could. He then commanded his general ... to draw up the troops in close order, and march them under me; the foot by twenty-four abreast, and the horse by sixteen, with drums beating, colours flying, and pikes advanced ... His majesty gave orders, upon pain of death, that every soldier in his march should observe the strictest decency with regard to my person; which however could not prevent some of the younger officers from turning up their eyes as they passed under me: and, to confess the truth, my breeches were at that time in so ill a condition, that they afforded some opportunities for laughter and admiration. [Chapter 3]

The two great empires of Lilliput and Blefuscu [have] been engaged in a most obstinate war for six-and-thirty moons past. It began upon the following occasion. It is allowed on all hands, that the primitive way of breaking eggs, before we eat them, was upon the larger end; but his present majesty's grandfather, while he was a boy, going to eat an egg, and breaking it according to the ancient practice, happened to cut one of his fingers. Whereupon the emperor his father published an edict, commanding all his subjects, upon great penalties, to break the smaller end of their eggs. The people so highly resented this law, that our histories tell us, there have been six rebellions raised on that account; wherein one emperor lost his life, and another his crown … It is computed that eleven thousand persons have at several times suffered death, rather than submit to break their eggs at the smaller end. [Chapter 4]

I shall say but little at present of their learning, which, for many ages, has flourished in all its branches among them: but their manner of writing is very peculiar, being neither from the left to the right, like the Europeans, nor from the right to the left, like the Arabians, nor from up to down, like the Chinese, but aslant, from one corner of the paper to the other, like ladies in England. [Chapter 6]

They bury their dead with their heads directly downwards, because they hold an opinion that in eleven thousand moons they are all to rise again, in which period the earth (which they conceive to be flat) will turn upside down, and by this means they shall, at their resurrection, be found ready standing on their feet. The learned among them confess the absurdity of this doctrine, but the practice still continues, in compliance to the vulgar. [Chapter 6]

Part II: A VOYAGE TO BROBDINGNAG

For the Queen (who had indeed but a weak stomach) took up at one mouthful as much as a dozen English farmers could eat at a meal, which to me was for some time a very nauseous sight. She would craunch the wing of a lark, bones and all, between her teeth, although it were nine times as large as that of a full-grown turkey; and put a bit of bread in her mouth, as big as two twelve-penny loaves.

She drank out of a golden cup, above a hogshead at a draught. Her knives were twice as long as a scythe set straight upon the handle. The spoons, forks, and other instruments were all in the same proportion. [Chapter 3]

The maids of honour often invited Glumdalclitch to their apartments, and desired she would bring me along with her, on purpose to have the pleasure of seeing and touching me. They would often strip me naked from top to toe, and lay me at full length in their bosoms; wherewith I was much disgusted because, to say the truth, a very offensive smell came from their skins; which I do not mention, or intend, to the disadvantage of those excellent ladies, for whom I have all manner of respect; but I conceive that my sense was more acute in proportion to my littleness, and that those illustrious persons were no more disagreeable to their lovers, or to each other, than people of the same quality are with us in England ... The handsomest among these maids of honour, a pleasant, frolicsome girl of sixteen, would sometimes set me astride upon one of her nipples, with many other tricks, wherein the reader will excuse me for not being over particular. But I was so much displeased, that I entreated Glumdalclitch to contrive some excuse for not seeing that young lady any more. [Chapter 5]

Great allowances should be given to a King who lives wholly secluded from the rest of the world, and must therefore be altogether unacquainted with the manners and customs that most prevail in other nations: the want of which knowledge will ever produce many prejudices, and a certain narrowness of thinking, from which we and the politer countries of Europe are wholly exempted. [Chapter 7]

Part III: A Voyage to Laputa, Balnibarbi, Glubbdubdrib, Luggnagg and Japan

They made signs for me to come down from the rock, and go towards the shore, which I accordingly did; and the flying island being raised to a convenient height, the verge directly over me, a chain was let down from the lowest gallery, with a seat fastened to the bottom, to which I fixed myself, and was drawn up by pulleys. [Chapter 1]

Their heads were all reclined either to the right, or the left; one of their eyes turned inward, and the other directly up to the zenith. Their outward garments were adorned with the figures of suns, moons, and stars, interwoven with those of fiddles, flutes, harps, trumpets, guitars, harpsichords, and many more instruments of music, unknown to us in Europe. I observed here and there many in the habit of servants, with a blown bladder fastened like a flail to the end of a short stick, which they carried in their hands. In each bladder was a small quantity of dried peas or little pebbles (as I was afterwards informed). With these bladders they now and then flapped the mouths and ears of those who stood near them, of which practice I could not then conceive the meaning; it seems, the minds of these people are so taken up with intense speculations, that they neither can speak, nor attend to the discourses of others, without being roused by some external taction [touch] upon the organs of speech and hearing. [Chapter 2]

I was received very kindly by the warden, and went for many days to the Academy. Every room has in it one or more projectors; and I believe I could not be in fewer than five hundred rooms.

The first man I saw was of a meagre aspect, with sooty hands and face, his hair and beard long, ragged, and singed in several places. His clothes, shirt, and skin, were all of the same colour. He has been eight years upon a project for extracting sunbeams out of cucumbers, which were to be put in phials hermetically sealed, and let out to warm the air in raw inclement summers ...

I went into another chamber, but was ready to hasten back, being almost overcome with a horrible stink ... The projector of this cell was the most ancient student of the Academy; his face and beard were of a pale yellow; his hands and clothes daubed over with filth. When I was presented to him, he gave me a close embrace, a compliment I could well have excused. His employment, from his first coming into the academy, was an operation to reduce human excrement to its original food, by separating the several parts, removing the tincture which it receives from the gall, making the odour exhale, and scumming off the saliva. He had a weekly allowance, from the society, of a vessel filled with human ordure, about the bigness of a Bristol barrel ...

There was a most ingenious architect, who had contrived a new method for building houses, by beginning at the roof, and working downward to the foundation; which he justified to me, by the like practice of those two prudent insects, the bee and the spider. [Chapter 5]

Part IV: A Voyage to the Country of the Houyhnhnms

I fell into a beaten road, where I saw many tracks of human feet, and some of cows, but most of horses. At last I beheld several animals in a field, and one or two of these same kind sitting in trees. Their shape was very singular, and deformed, which a little discomposed me, so that I lay down behind a thicket to observe them better ... Their heads and breasts were covered with a thick hair, some frizzled and others lank; they had beards like goats, and a long ridge of hair down their backs, and the foreparts of their legs and feet, but the rest of their bodies were bare, so that I might see their skins, which were of a brown buff colour. They had no tails, nor any hair at all on their buttocks, except about the anus; which, I presume, Nature had placed there to defend them as they sat on the ground; for this posture they used, as well as lying down, and often stood on their hind feet. [Chapter 1]

[Among the Houyhnhnms] I enjoyed perfect health of body and tranquillity of mind; I did not feel the treachery or inconstancy of a friend, nor the injuries of a secret or open enemy. I had no occasion of bribing, flatting or pimping, to procure the favour of any great man or of his minion. I wanted no fence against fraud or oppression; here was neither physician to destroy my body, nor lawyer to ruin my fortune; no informer to watch my words and actions, or forge accusations against me for hire: here were no gibers, censurers, backbiters, pickpockets, highwaymen, housebreakers, attorneys, bawds, buffoons, gamesters, politicians, wits, splenetics, tedious talkers, controvertists, ravishers, murderers, robbers, virtuosos; no leaders or followers of party and faction; no encouragers to vice, by seducement or examples: no dungeon, axes, gibbets, whipping posts, or pillories; no cheating shopkeepers or mechanics: no pride, vanity, or affectation: no fops, bullies, drunkards, strolling whores, or poxes: no ranting, lewd, expensive wives: no stupid proud pendants: no importunate, overbearing, quarrelsome, noisy, roaring, empty, conceited, swearing companions: no scoundrels, raised from the dust upon the merit of their vices, or nobility thrown into it on account of their virtues: no Lords, fiddlers, judges or dancing-masters. [Chapter 10]

When I thought of my family, my friends, my countrymen, or the human race in general, I considered them, as they really were,

Yahoos in shape and disposition, perhaps a little more civilized, and qualified with the gift of speech; but making no other use of reason, than to improve and multiply those vices whereof their brethren in this country had only the share that nature allotted them. When I happened to behold the reflection of my own form in a lake or fountain, I turned away my face in horror and detestation of myself, and could better endure the sight of a common Yahoo than of my own person. By conversing with the Houyhnhnms, and looking upon them with delight, I fell to imitate their gait and gesture, which is now grown into a habit; and my friends often tell me, in a blunt way, that I trot like a horse; which, however, I take for a great compliment. [Chapter 10]

I began last week to permit my wife to sit at dinner with me, at the farthest end of a long table; and to answer (but with the utmost brevity) the few questions I asked her. Yet, the smell of a Yahoo continuing very offensive, I always keep my nose well stopped with rue, lavender, or tobacco leaves. [Chapter 12]

J. S. Müller. inv: del: et Se.

Part the Sixth:

DISOBLIGING ENGLAND.

BEING

A

GALLIMAUFRY OF OPUSCULES

from the later

Prose & Poetry

of the

WRITER

acclaimed in his native City

as

the 'Drapier',

& throughout the whole

Civilized World

as

Dean Swift.

From My Lady's Lamentation & Complaint against the Dean

Swift's 'truest, most virtuous and valuable friend' was no more, but life went on. In June 1728, he was invited for the first time to visit the Achesons, Sir Arthur and Lady Anne, at Market Hill, their estate in County Armagh. He spent much of his time there out of doors, building pigsties, catching rats, pruning trees, working in the dairy and overseeing landscaping work in the garden. Among the many 'little amusing improvements' he added to the grounds were two outdoor privies – much needed amenities, as he makes plain in a long poem written in what he called 'Lilliputian verse', which includes the following lines:

… How proudly he talks
Of zigzags and walks;
And all the day raves
Of cradles and caves;
And boasts of his feats,
His grottoes and seats;
Shows all the gewgaws,   [curiosities
And gapes for applause!
A fine occupation
For one of his station!

A hole where a rabbît

Would scorn to inhabît,

Dug out in an hour —

He calls ît a bower ...

The girls of the village

Come flocking for pillage,

Pull down the fine briers

And thorns to make fires;

But yet are so kind

To leave something behind:

No more need be said on't,

I smell when I tread on't ...

LADY ACHESON WEARY OF THE DEAN

On that visît, the firſt of several, Swift remained in Market Hill for some eight months, until February 1729. Anne Acheson's lively mind (in a painfully thin and frail body) helped to fill the gap left by the death of Stella, and briefly brought laughter and bantering back into his life. He imagined her complaining to her husband about him:

The Dean would visit Market Hill,
Our invitation was but slight;
I said, 'Why let him, if he will.'
And so I bade Sir Arthur write.

His manners would not let him wait,
Lest we should think ourselves neglected,
And so we see him at our gate
Three days before he was expected.

After a week, a month, a quarter,
And day succeeding after day,
Says not a word of his departure,
Though not a soul would have him stay.

I've said enough to make him blush,
Methinks, or else the devil's in't;
But he cares not for it a rush,
Nor for my life will take the hint.

But you, my life, may let him know,
In civil language, if he stays,
How deep and foul the roads may grow,
And that he may command the chaise.

Or you may say, 'My wife intends,
Though I should be exceeding proud,
This winter to invîte some friends,
And, sir, I know you hate a crowd.'

Or, 'Mr Dean, I should wîth joy
Beg you would here continue ſtill,
But we muſt go to Aghnacloy,
Or Mr Moore will take ît ill.'

The house accounts are daily riſing;
So much his ſtay doth swell the bills:
My deareſt life, ît is surprising
How much he eats, how much he swills.

His brace of puppies, how they ſtuff,
And they muſt have three meals a day,
Yet never think they get enough;
His horses too eat all our hay.

O, if I could, how I would maul
His tallow face and wainscot paws,
His beetle brows, and eyes of wall,
And make him soon ǵive up the cause!

Must I be every moment chid   [chided

With 'Skinnybonia', 'Snipe', and 'Lean'?

O that I could but once be rid

Of that insulting tyrant Dean!

Twelve Articles

Modelled perhaps on the '39 Articles' in the Book of Common Prayer, these pointed rules emerged from Swift's dealings with the feisty Lady Acheson. As he wrote to Thomas Sheridan: 'My Lady is perpetually quarrelling with Sir Arthur and me, and shews every creature the libels I have writ against her.' In fact Anne Acheson was so pleased with what Swift was saying about her that she collected his new verses together in an album. Though, in reality, 'Twelve Articles' is composed of teasing insults, it pretends to be a list of rules dictating how two incompatible people of opposite sexes might manage to keep the peace — an eighteenth-century *Men are from Mars, Women are from Venus*.

I. Lest it may more quarrels breed, I will never hear you read.

II. By disputing, I will never,
    To convince you once endeavour.

III. When a paradox you stick to,
    I will never contradict you.

IV. When I talk and you are heedless,
    I will show no anger needless.

V. When your speeches are absurd,
    I will ne'er object a word.

VI. When you furious argue wrong,
    I will grieve and hold my tongue.

VII. Not a jest or humorous story
    Will I ever tell before ye:
    To be chidden for explaining,   [scolded
    When you quite mistake the meaning.

VIII. Never more will I suppose,
    You can taste my verse or prose.   [appreciate

IX. You no more at me shall fret,
    While I teach and you forget.

X. You shall never hear me thunder,
    When you blunder on, and blunder.

XI. Show your poverty of spirit,
   And in dress place all your merit;
   Give yourself ten thousand airs:
   That with me shall break no squares.   [do no harm

XII. Never will I give advice,
   Till you please to ask me thrice:
   Which if you in scorn reject,
   'Twill be just as I expect.

   Thus we both shall have our ends,
   And continue special friends.

From A MODEST PROPOSAL

FOR PREVENTING THE CHILDREN OF POOR PEOPLE FROM BEING A BURDEN TO THEIR PARENTS OR THE COUNTRY, AND FOR MAKING THEM BENEFICIAL TO THE PUBLIC.

In the autumn of 1729, Swift at last came home from Armagh. He was met on the outskirts of the city by great crowds of Dubliners, rich and poor, accompanied by musicians, balladeers and the inevitable beggars. Bonfires were lit, bells were rung, and people got drunk. No one had forgotten that some five years before, he had been 'M.B. Drapier', the pamphleteer whose intervention convinced the public to resist the English establishment's intention to flood Ireland with almost worthless coinage ('Wood's Halfpence'), and successfully scuppered the scheme. Swift had seriously risked imprisonment, proving himself a true national patriot: he was now a popular hero.

That October, 'A Modest Proposal', his most famous satire, appeared anonymously in the *Dublin Intelligence*. Its savagery echoed what the Dean had seen of the squalid conditions around him in Dublin and throughout the country.

Proposing with apparent sincerity and logic a horrifying solution to the plight of the Irish poor, the speaker attacks both the maladministration of governance under the Crown and the problem of rapacious native landlords.

It is a melancholy object to those who walk through this great town, or travel in the country, when they see the streets, the roads, and cabin doors crowded with beggars of the female sex, followed by three, four, or six children, all in rags, and importuning every passenger [passer-by] for an alms. These mothers, instead of being able to work for their honest livelihood, are forced to employ all their time in strolling to beg sustenance for their helpless infants who, as they grow up, either turn thieves for want of work, or leave their dear native country to fight for the Pretender [James Stuart, son of James II] in Spain, or sell themselves to the Barbadoes [as servants on sugar plantations] ... The number of souls in this kingdom being usually reckoned one million and a half, of these I calculate there may be about two hundred thousand couples whose wives are breeders; from which number I subtract thirty thousand couples who are able to maintain their own children, although I apprehend there cannot be so many, under the present distresses of the kingdom; but this being granted, there will remain a hundred and seventy thousand breeders.

I again subtract fifty thousand for those women who miscarry, or whose children die by accident or disease within the year. There only remain a hundred and twenty thousand children of poor parents annually born ... I shall now therefore humbly propose my own thoughts, which I hope will not be liable to the least objection.

I have been assured by a very knowing American of my acquaintance in London, that a young healthy child, well nursed, is at a year old a most delicious, nourishing, and wholesome food, whether stewed, roasted, baked or boiled; and I make no doubt that it will equally serve in a fricassee or a ragout.

I do therefore humbly offer it to public consideration that of the hundred and twenty thousand children already computed, twenty thousand may be reserved for breed, whereof only one fourth part to be males, which is more than we allow to sheep, black cattle or swine; and my reason is that these children are seldom the fruits of marriage, a circumstance not much regarded by our savages; therefore one male will be sufficient to serve four females. That the remaining hundred thousand may, at a year old, be offered in sale to the persons of quality and fortune through the kingdom; always advising the mother to let them suck plentifully in the last month, so as to render them plump and fat for a good table. A child will make two dishes at an entertainment for friends; and when the family dines alone, the fore or hind quarter will make a reasonable dish, and seasoned with a little pepper or salt will be very good boiled on the fourth day, especially in winter ... I grant this food will be somewhat dear, and therefore very proper for landlords, who, as they have already devoured most of the parents, seem to have the best title to the children ... Those who are more thrifty (as I must confess the times require) may flay the carcass; the skin of which artificially dressed will make admirable gloves for ladies, and summer boots for fine gentlemen.

As to our city of Dublin, shambles [slaughterhouses] may be appointed for this purpose in the most convenient parts of it, and butchers we may be assured will not be wanting; although I rather recommend buying the children alive, and dressing them hot from the knife, as we do roasting pigs ...

I think the advantages by the proposal which I have made are obvious and many, as well as of the highest importance.

For first, ... it would greatly lessen the number of Papists, with whom we are yearly overrun, being the principal breeders of the nation as well as our most dangerous enemies; and who stay at home on purpose with a design to deliver the kingdom to the Pretender, hoping to take their advantage by the absence of so many good Protestants, who have chosen rather to leave their country than stay at home and pay tithes against their conscience to an episcopal curate.

Secondly, the poorer tenants will have something valuable of their own, which by law may be made liable to distress and help to pay their landlord's rent, their corn and cattle being already seized, and money a thing unknown.

Thirdly, whereas the maintenance of a hundred thousand children, from two years old and upward, cannot be computed at less than ten shillings apiece per annum, the nation's stock will be thereby increased fifty thousand pounds per annum, beside the profit of a new dish introduced to the tables of all gentlemen of fortune in the kingdom who have any refinement in taste; and the money will circulate among ourselves, the goods being entirely of our own growth and manufacture.

Fourthly, the constant breeders, beside the gain of eight shillings sterling per annum by the sale of their children, will be rid of the charge of maintaining them after the first year.

Fifthly, this food would likewise bring great custom to taverns, where the vintners will certainly be so prudent as to procure the best receipts for dressing it to perfection, and consequently have their houses frequented by all the fine gentlemen, who justly value themselves upon their knowledge in good eating; and a skilful cook, who understands how to oblige his guests, will contrive to make it as expensive as they please.

Sixthly, this would be a great inducement to marriage, which all wise nations have either encouraged by rewards or enforced by laws and penalties. It would increase the care and tenderness of mothers toward their children, when they were sure of a settlement for life to the poor babes, provided in some sort by the public to their annual profit instead of expense. We should see an honest emulation among the married women, which of them could bring the fattest child to the market. Men would become as fond of their wives during the time of their pregnancy as they are now of their mares in foal, their cows in calf, their sows when they are ready to farrow; nor offer to beat or kick them (as is too frequent a practice) for fear of a miscarriage ...

As to myself, having been wearied out for many years with offering vain, idle, visionary thoughts, and at length utterly despairing of success, I fortunately fell upon this proposal; which, as it is wholly new, so it hath something solid and real, of no expense and little trouble, full in our own power, and whereby we can incur no danger in disobliging England. For this kind of commodity will not bear exportation, and flesh being of too tender a consistence to admit a long continuance in salt, although perhaps I could name a country which would be glad to eat up our whole nation without it.

VERSES MADE FOR THE WOMEN WHO CRY APPLES, ETC.

Swift loved fruit, but always tried to avoid it, believing that the giddiness and deafness that plagued him throughout his adult life had been caused by eating 'a hundred golden pippins' from Sir William Temple's garden. As Dean, he knew many of the traders in the streets around the Cathedral, and used to overpay when he bought from them. His friend Dr Delany later recalled his 'seraglio' of impoverished and crippled ladies: 'One of these mistresses sold plums; another, hob-nails; a third tapes; a fourth, gingerbread; a fifth, knitted; a sixth, darned stockings; and a seventh, cobbled shoes; and so on, beyond my counting … insomuch that there was scarce one street, or alley, or lane in Dublin, its suburbs, and its environs, that had not at least one or more of them.' Swift was so fascinated by their sales pitches that he composed a number of street cries for them himself …

APPLES

Come buy my fine wares,
Plums, apples and pears.
A hundred a penny,
In conscience too many:
Come, will you have any?
My children are seven,
I wish them in Heaven;
My husband's a sot,
With his pipe and his pot,
Not a farthing will gain 'em,
And I must maintain 'em.

ASPARAGUS

Ripe 'sparagrass,
Fit for lad or lass,
To make their water pass:
O, 'tis a pretty picking
With a tender chicken.

Onions

Come, follow me by the smell,
Here's delicate onions to sell;
I promise to use you well.
They make the blood warmer,
You'll feed like a farmer;
For this is every cook's opinion,
No savoury dish whout an onion;
But, left your kissing should be spoiled,
Your onions must be thoroughly boiled:
Or else you may spare
Your mistress a share,
The secret will never be known:
She cannot discover
The breath of her lover,
But think it as sweet as her own.

Oysters

Charming oysters I cry,
My masters come buy,
So plump and so fresh,
So sweet is their flesh,
No Colchester oyster,

Is sweeter and moister,
Your stomach they settle,
And rouse up your mettle,
They'll make you a dad
Of a lass or a lad;
And Madam your wife
They'll please to the life;
Be she barren, be she old,
Be she slut, or be she scold,
Eat my oysters, and lie near her,
She'll be fruitful, never fear her.

HERRINGS

Be not sparing,
Leave off swearing,
Buy my herring
Fresh from Malahide,
Better ne'er was tried.
Come, eat 'em with pure fresh butter and mustard,
Their bellies are soft, and as white as a custard.
Come, sixpence a dozen, to get me some bread,
Or, like my own herrings, I soon shall be dead.

ORANGES

Come, buy my fine oranges, sauce for your veal,

And charming when squeezed in a pot of brown ale.

Well roasted, with sugar and wine in a cup,

They'll make a sweet bishop when gentlefolks sup.

[a drink, such as spiced port

From THE LADY'S DRESSING ROOM

Laetîtia Pilkington, a scholar and poet who saw much of
Swift in the 1730s, said that these verses displayed 'all the
dirtiest ideas in the world in one piece'. In her *Memoirs* she
remarked: 'With all the reverence I have for the Dean, I
really think he sometimes chose subjects unworthy of his
muse, and which could serve no other end except that of
turning the reader's stomach, as it did my mother's, who
upon reading the *Lady's Dressing Room*, instantly threw up her
dinner.' The poem, which is perhaps an answer in part to
his friend Alexander Pope's 'The Rape of the Lock', is one
of a series often known as the 'filthy poems', written about
three years after the death of Stella. The names 'Strephon'
and 'Celia' are found in innocent romantic and pastoral
poetry; these two (particularly Strephon, whose motives
appear to be decidedly sleazy) are anything but innocent.

Five hours, (and who can do it less in?)
By haughty Celia ſpent in dressing;
The goddess from her chamber issues,
Arrayed in lace, brocades and tissues.
Strephon, who found the room was void,
And Betty otherwise employed,
Stole in, and took a ſtrict survey,
Of all the litter as it lay;
Whereof, to make the matter clear,
An inventory follows here:

And firſt a dirty smock appeared,
Beneath the armpits well besmeared.
Strephon, the rogue, diſplayed it wide,
And turned it round on every side.
On such a point few words are beſt,
And Strephon bids us guess the reſt,
But swears how damnably the men lie,
In calling Celia sweet and cleanly.

Now liſten while he next produces
The various combs for various uses,
Filled up with dirt so closely fixed,
No brush could force a way betwixt.

A paste of composition rare,

Sweat, dandruff, powder, lead and hair;

A forehead cloth with oil upon't

To smooth the wrinkles on her front;

Here alum flower to stop the steams,   [chemical powder

Exhaled from sour unsavoury streams,

There night-gloves made of Tripsy's hide,   [Celia's pet dog

Bequeathed by Tripsy when she died,

With puppy water, beauty's help

        [a moisturiser made from boiled puppy

Distilled from Tripsy's darling whelp;

Here gallipots and vials placed,   [cosmetic jars

Some filled with washes, some with paste,

Some with pomatum, paints and slops,   [scented creams

And ointments good for scabby chops.

Hard by a filthy basin stands,

Fouled with the scouring of her hands;

The basin takes whatever comes

The scrapings of her teeth and gums,

A nasty compound of all hues,

For here she spits, and here she spews.

But oh! it turned poor Strephon's bowels

When he beheld and smelled the towels,

Begummed, bemattered, and beslimed

With dirt, and sweat, and earwax grimed.

No object Strephon's eye escapes,

Here petticoats in frowzy heaps;

Nor be the handkerchiefs forgot

All varnished o'er with snuff and snot.

The stockings why should I expose,

Stained with the marks of stinking toes;

Or greasy coifs and pinners reeking,   [types of nightcap

Which Celia slept at least a week in?

A pair of tweezers next he found

To pluck her brows in arches round,

Or hairs that sink the forehead low,

Or on her chin like bristles grow ...

Why Strephon will you tell the rest?

And must you needs describe the chest? ...

                    [do you *have* to describe the commode?

He lifts the lid, there needs no more,

He smelled it all the time before ...

O never may such vile machine

Be once in Celia's chamber seen!

O may she better learn to keep

Those 'secrets of the hoary deep!' ...   [Milton – the ocean

So things, which must not be expressed,
When plumped into the reeking chest,   [plopped
Send up an excremental smell
To taint the parts from whence they fell;
The petticoats and gown perfume,
Which waft a stink round every room.

Thus finishing his grand survey,
Disgusted Strephon stole away
Repeating in his amorous fits,
'Oh! Celia, Celia, Celia shits!' . . .

J.J.Müller inv. del. et Sc:

Part the Seventh:

THE DEAN BEGINS TO BREAK.

BEING

an ultimate choice of

THREE MEMORIAL EXTRACTS

from the works of the late

Doctor Swift,

the same being illustrative alike of

his **WIT,**

his **UNDERSTANDING**

& his

COURAGE.

A REVEREND DEAN'S LAMENTATION FOR THE LOSS OF HIS HEARING

Swift had been hoping to make a farewell visit to England in 1734, but after a renewed attack of his inner ear disorder in September, he realised that was never going to happen. When his housekeeper found a sheet of paper bearing these lines on his desk, he told her to take it away. Within a few days, the poem had appeared in the *Dublin Evening Post*.

Deaf, giddy, helpless, left alone,
To all my friends a burden grown;
No more I hear my parish bell,
Than if it rang for my own knell:
At thunder, now, no more I start,
Than at the rumbling of a cart;
And what's incredible, alack!
No more I hear a woman's clack.

From VERSES ON THE DEATH OF DR SWIFT

Swift's best-known poem was first published in Dublin in 1739, though it was written some years earlier. It was inspired by a maxim by the French literary grandee, La Rochefoucauld: 'In the misfortune of our best friends, we find something that does not displease us.' In the first part of the work, Swift imagines how friends and acquaintances will react to the news of his death; in the second part, we overhear someone speaking fulsomely about the character of the late Dean. Here too, as we have come to expect, there is irony, for of course the person doing this 'objective obituary' is Swift himself, scarcely the most impartial witness. Yet another level of irony may be added when one reflects that posterity has tended to agree with him.

... The time is not remote, when I
Must by the course of nature die;
When I foresee my special friends
Will try to find their private ends:
Though it is hardly understood
Which way my death can do them good,
Yet thus, methinks, I hear 'em speak:

'See, how the Dean begins to break:

Poor gentleman, he droops apace!

You plainly find it in his face:

That old vertigo in his head   [pronounced 'verteego'

Will never leave him, till he's dead.

Besides, his memory decays:

He recollects not what he says;

He cannot call his friends to mind;

Forgets the place where last he dined;

Plies you with stories o'er and o'er;

He told them fifty times before ...

Behold the fatal day arrive!

'How is the Dean?' — 'He's just alive.'

Now the departing prayer is read:

'He hardly breathes.' — 'The Dean is dead.'

Before the passing-bell begun,   [death-bell

The news through half the town has run:

'O, may we all for death prepare!

What has he left, and who's his heir?'

'I know no more than what the news is;

'Tis all bequeathed to public uses.'

'To public use! A perfect whim!

What had the public done for him? ...'

From Dublin soon to London spread,
'Tis told at court, 'The Dean is dead ...'
The Queen, so gracious, mild, and good,
Cries, 'Is he gone! 'Tis time he should.
He's dead, you say; why, let him rot;
I'm glad the meadels were forgot ...'   [medals she offered Swift
Here shift the scene, to represent
How those I love my death lament:
Poor Pope will grieve a month, and Gay
A week, and Arbuthnot a day ...   [fellow Scriblerians
My female friends, whose tender hearts
Have better learned to act their parts,
Receive the news in doleful dumps:
'The Dean is dead (*and what is trumps?*)
Then, Lord have mercy on his soul!
(*Ladies, I'll venture for the vole.*)   [try to win all the tricks at cards
Six deans, they say, must bear the pall
(*I wish I knew which king to call.*) ...
His time was come: he ran his race;
We hope he's in a better place.' ...

One year is past; a different scene;
No further mention of the Dean;
Who now, alas, no more is missed,
Than if he never did exist ...

Some country squire to Lintot goes,　[a London bookseller
Inquires for *Swift in Verse and Prose*.
Says Lintot, 'I have heard the name;
He died a year ago.' 'The same.'
He searches all his shop in vain:
'Sir, you may find them in Duck Lane;　[for unwanted books
I sent them with a load of books,
Laſt Monday to the paſtry-cook's ...　[for wrapping pies, *etc.*
The Dean was famous in his time,
And had a kind of knack at rhyme ...'

Suppose me dead; and then suppose
A club assembled at the Rose;　　　　　[a tavern
Where, from discourse of this and that,
I grow the subjeƈt of their chat
And, while they toss my name about,
With favour some, and some without;
One, quite indifferent in the cause,
My charaƈter impartial draws:

'The Dean, if we believe report,
Was never ill received at court.
As for his works in verse and prose
I own myself no judge of those;

Nor can I tell what critics thought 'em:

But this I know, all people bought 'em.

As with a moral view designed

To cure the vices of mankind:

His vein, ironically grave,

Exposed the fool, and lashed the knave ...

'With princes kept a due decorum,

But never stood in awe before 'em,

And to her Majesty, God bless her,

Would speak as free as to her dresser:

She thought it his peculiar whim,

Nor took it ill as come from him.

He followed David's lesson just: [from Psalm 146

In princes never put thy trust ...

'Fair Liberty was all his cry,

For her he stood prepared to die;

For her he boldly stood alone;

For her he oft exposed his own.

Two kingdoms, just as faction led,

Had set a price upon his head;

But not a traitor could be found

To sell him for six hundred pound ...

'But, finding vain was all his care,

He left the court in mere despair ...   [total

Pursued by base, envenomed pens

Far to the land of slaves and fens;

A servile race in folly nursed,

Who truckle most, when treated worst ...   [concede

'Perhaps I may allow, the Dean

Had too much satire in his vein;

And seemed determined not to starve it,

Because no age could more deserve it.

Yet malice never was his aim;

He lashed the vice, but spared the name ...

'He gave the little wealth he had

To build a house for fools and mad;

                    [St Patrick's Hospital, opened 1757

And showed by one satiric touch,

No nation wanted it so much.

That kingdom he hath left his debtor,

I wish it soon may have a better.'

SWIFT'S EPITAPH

The last five years of Swift's life were increasingly miserable. Deaf, often in pain and erratic in temper, he spent his days alone, walking the Deanery stairs. For much of the time, he hardly spoke. Among his last recorded utterances were the words, 'I am what I am,' repeated over and over again, and on another occasion, 'I am a fool.'

On 19 October 1745, he died. Visitors came to pay their respects, and snipped off locks of his white hair. He was buried in St Patrick's Cathedral, where the epitaph he wrote for himself may be visited. This is a literal translation.

Here is placed the Body of
Jonathan Swift, Doctor of Sacred Theology,
Of this Cathedral Church
Dean,
Where savage Indignation
No more
Can lacerate his Heart.
Depart, Traveller,
And if you are able, imitate this man
Who, using all the strength he had,
Was the Defender of Liberty.

A Note on the Illustration & Design

This book, celebrating Dr Jonathan Swift, also takes inspiration from the period of his writing in its appearance.

The illustrations are largely from *The Works of Dr. Jonathan Swift, Vol 1., 1760* (of Twelve Volumes). These beautiful and intricate copperplate prints, by J.S. Müller, seem to fit the period feel of the book, and are a happy match with the chapter titles.

I have used ligatures in the text where possible as, again, it fits the period. A ligature occurs where two or more elements of a single letterform are joined as one. So 'it' becomes it, 'st' becomes st, etc. The use of ligatures, in printing, came from their use in handwriting, but eventually died out after the eighteenth century, in both printed and handwritten texts. Charlotte Bronte wrote *Jane Eyre* with the medial 's' or ʃ, something that could not be read easily today (which is why it is the only ligature I have omitted). The ampersand '&' is a ligature still in use, coming from the latin 'et'.

During the eighteenth century, there were two large type foundries in Britain, those of William Caslon and John Baskerville. The font used in this book is Mrs Eaves, called after John Baskerville's mistress and later wife, Sarah Eaves, herself a printer of type, and designed by Zuzana Licko in 1996. I used it because of its connection to these great foundries and for its many beautiful ligatures, and non-aligning numerals.

Emma Byrne

ACKNOWLEDGEMENTS

Probably my greatest debt is to my parents, Robert and Lois Wyse Jackson, whose interest in Jonathan Swift I imbibed from an early age. I am also grateful to the following, all of whom helped in various ways in the preparation of this book: Althea Farren, the late Fr Matt Glynn, Dr Patrick Wyse Jackson, Dr Peter van de Kamp and, as ever, my wife, Ruth.

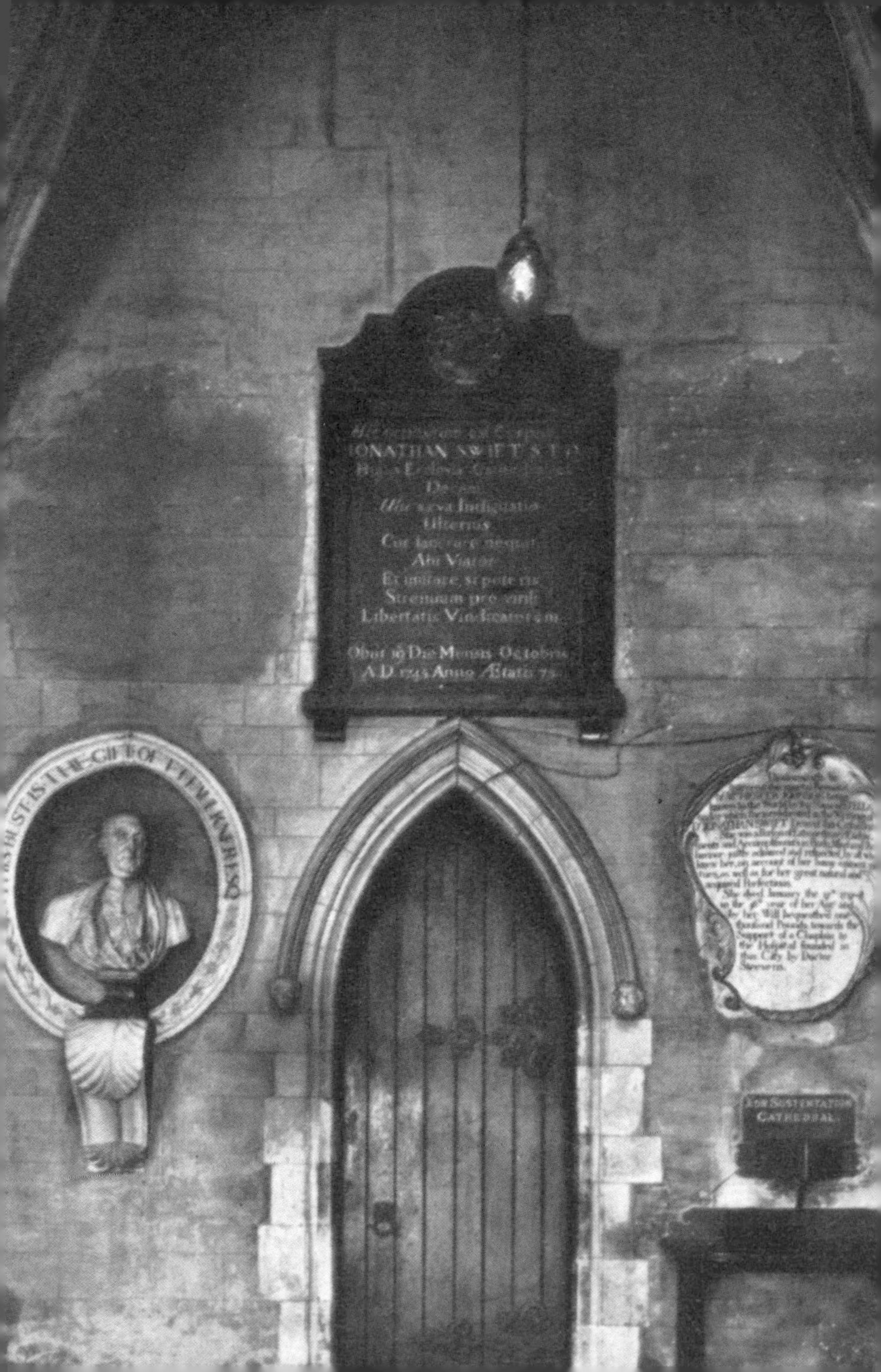
JONATHAN SWIFT S.T.D.
Abi Viator
Libertatis Vindicatorem.
FOR SUSTENTATION
CATHEDRAL